ORATION ON THE DIGNITY
OF MAN

GIOVANNI PICO DELLA MIRANDOLA

ORATION
ON THE DIGNITY OF MAN

Translated by A. Robert Caponigri

A Gateway Edition
REGNERY PUBLISHING, INC.
WASHINGTON, D.C.

1999 printing.

International Standard Book Number: 0-89526-713-6

Library of Congress Cataloging-in-Publication Data

Published in the United States by
Regnery Publishing, Inc.
An Eagle Publishing Company
One Massachusetts Avenue, NW
Washington, DC 20001

Printed on acid-free paper.
Manufactured in the United States of America

10 9 8 7 6

Books are available in quantity for promotional or premium use. Write to
Director of Special Sales, Regnery Publishing, Inc., One Massachusetts
Avenue, NW, Washington, DC 20001, for information on discounts and terms
or call (202) 216-0600.

CONTENTS

TRANSLATOR'S NOTE

This "most elegant oration" (*oratio elegantissima*) as it was called in the first edition of the collected works and as it has been named ever since, of Giovanni Pico, Count of Mirandola (1463-1494) was composed as a prelusion to the disputation which Mirandola proposed to hold shortly after Epiphany, 1487. In this disputation, as he recounts in the course of the "Oration," Pico proposed to defend nine hundred propositions. The disputation did not take place because it was suspended by Pope Innocentius VIII, who also appointed a commission to examine the theses. Some of them were condemned as counter to the accepted teachings. In reply Pico composed an *Apology*, in the course of which he reproduced the second portion of the "Oratio" practically *verbatim*. This is, consequently, the first appearance of the "Oratio," or any part of it in public print. The whole of the "Oratio" was first published in the collection of Pico's works edited and published by his relative, Gian Francesco Pico, in 1496. The qualifying phrase "on the dignity of man" is a later addition, but has become practically identical with the oration, even though some writers have protested that it has reference only to the first portion. Subsequent editions of the *Opera Omnia* in which the "Oratio" is included appeared at Venice in 1498; at Strasburg in 1504; at Reggio in 1506; at Paris 1505; again at Venice in 1519 and 1557; and at Basel in 1530, 1537, 1557 and 1572. Numerous editions of the "Oratio" alone have appeared since that time. The present translation is based conjointly on one of the most recent and best of these individual editions, that of Bruno Cicognani (Giovanni Pico della Mirandola: *Dignita dell'uomo (De hominis dignitate)*, Testo, Traduzione e Note, Firenze, Le Monnier 3a ed., 1941), and the text of *Opera Omnia* of 1504. A German translation appeared in a selection of Pico's writings edited and translated by Arthur Liebert (Arthur Liebert: *Giovanni Pico della Mirandola: Ausgewaehlte Schriften*, Jena und Leipzig, 1905); in Italian a translation by Semprini (Giovanni Semprini: *La filosofia di Pico della Mirandola*, Milano, 1936 appendice), as well as that by Cicognani already referred to. In English, a translation by Charles G. Wallis was published in the magazine *View* (fall, 1944 and December, 1944). Several passages were translated and published in the *Journal of the History of Ideas* in 1942. This translation is by Elizabeth L. Forbes, who subsequently published an excellent complete translation in the volume *The Renaissance Philosophy of Man* edited by Ernst Cassirer, Paul Oscar Kristeller and John Herman Randell, Chicago, the University of Chicago Press, 1948. While the present translator has consulted all of these, the translation here offered is a fresh one, based directly on a reading of the Latin text as indicated above. Whatever merits or shortcomings it may have are consequently to be judged on this basis. His aim has been first, of course, adherence to the ideas; but he has also tried to reproduce something of the stylistic flavor of Pico.

INTRODUCTION

"The enduring value of Pico's work is due, not to his Quixotic quest of an accord between Pagan, Hebrew, and Christian traditions," John Addington Symonds writes, "but to the noble spirit of confidence and humane sympathy with all great movements of the mind, which penetrates it." Out of the bulk of the works of Count Giovanni Pico della Mirandola, who challenged the doctors of the schools to dispute with him on nine hundred grave questions, the only production widely read nowadays is this brief discourse, "The Dignity of Man," delivered by him in 1486, at Rome, when he was only twenty-four years old. The oration, which was his glove dashed down before authority, lives as the most succinct expression of the mind of the Renaissance.

Pico, a son of the princely house of Mirandola, one of the most brilliant of the great Renaissance families, studied at Bologna, and wandered through the Italian and French universities for seven years, becoming immensely erudite, proficient in Greek, Latin, Hebrew, Chaldee, and Arabic. Mystic, magician, and grand scholar, he combined in his character the Gothic complexity of the Middle Ages with the egoism and enlightenment of the Renaissance. He was the most romantic of all the Humanists. His immense design it was to effect a synthesis and reconciliation of Hebrew, classical, and Christian traditions. No one did more than Pico to restore Plato to dignity in the schools; yet, as Symonds observes, "uncontrolled by critical insight, and paralyzed by the prestige attaching to antiquity, the Florentine school [which Pico and Ficino dominated] produced little better than an unintelligent eclecticism." Among Pico's nine hundred questions were some propositions which hung close upon the brink of heresy. He thought that the secrets of the magicians could prove the divinity of Christ, and that the Cabala of the medieval Jews would sustain the Christian mysteries. Thus, haranguing, reading, wandering, preaching, commencing a vast work against the enemies of Christianity, he spent his brief life, dying of a fever before he was thirty—though he already had abjured the world and the flesh, and planned to wander barefoot as an evangelist.

Now this eccentric genius' "Dignity of Man" is the manifesto of humanism. Man regenerate—"this, visibly," Egon Freidell says, "is the primary meaning of the Renaissance: the rebirth of man in the likeness of God." The man of the Middle Ages was humble, conscious almost always of his fallen and sinful nature, feeling himself a miserable foul creature watched by an angry God. Through Pride fell the angels. But Pico and his brother-humanists declared that man was only a little lower than the angels, a being capable of descending to unclean depths, indeed, but also having it within his power to become godlike. How marvellous and splendid a creature is man! This is the theme of Pico's oration, elaborated with all the pomp and confidence that characterized the rising Humanist teachers. "In this idea," continues Freidell, "there lay a colossal *hybris* unknown to the Middle Ages, but also a tremendous spiritual impulse such as only modern times can show."

The very Cherubim and Seraphim must endure the equality of man, if Man cultivates his intellectual faculty. It is the spirit, the spark of Godhood, which raises Man above all the rest of creation and makes him distinct in kind from all other living things. For all his glorification of Man, however, Pico has no touch of the modern notion that "man makes himself," and that an honest God's the noblest work of man. It is only because Man has been created in the image of God that Man is angelic. God, in his generosity, has said to Man, "We have made thee neither of heaven or of earth, neither mortal nor immortal, so that with freedom of choice and with honor, as though the maker and moulder of thyself, thou mayest fashion thyself in whatever shape thou shalt prefer. Thou shalt have the power to degenerate into the lower forms of life, which are brutish. Thou shalt have the power, out of thy soul's judgment, to be reborn into the higher forms, which are divine."

This, then, is the essence of humanism, which spread out of Italy unto the whole of Europe, reaching its culmination, perhaps, in Erasmus and Sir Thomas More. (More it was who translated the life of Pico by his nephew Giovanni Francisco into English.) God had given Man great powers, and with those powers, free will. Man might rightfully take pride in his higher nature, and turn his faculties to the praise and improvement of noble human nature. A world of wonder and discovery lay before the Renaissance humanist. Yet all this dignity of human nature was the gift of God: the spiritual and rational powers neglected—and through free will Man is all too able to neglect them—Man sinks to the level of the brutes. The humanist does not seek to dethrone God: instead, through the moral disciplines of *humanitas,* he aspires to struggle upward toward the Godhead.

Thus a degree of humility chastened the pride of even the most arrogant humanist of the Renaissance. But the seed of *hubris,* overweening self-confidence, was sown; and a time would come when Man would take himself for the be-all and end-all; and then Nemesis would be felt once more, and —— The end, however, is not yet. It has remained for us of the twentieth century to look back upon the course of this *hubris,* diffused over all the world; and to see the oratorical aspirations of the humanists transformed into the technological aspirations of the modern sensual man; and to glimpse the beginning of the Catastrophe, perhaps, in a handful of dust over Hiroshima, or in the leaden domination of the Soviets, or in the pornography and hysteria of the corner news-stand. Robert Jungk, in *Tomorrow Is Already Here,* describes the stage of this progress at which we have arrived: "The stake is the throne of God.

To occupy God's place, to repeat His deeds, to recreate and organize a man-made cosmos according to man-made laws of reason, foresight, and efficiency"—this is the ambition of the twentieth-century energumen of progress. And to gratify this ambition, we have moved very near to the dehumanization of Man. In our lust for divine power, we have forgotten human dignity.

By "the dignity of man," Pico della Mirandola meant the high nobility of disciplined reason and imagination, human nature as redeemed by Christ, the uplifting of the truly human person through an exercise of soul and mind. He did not mean a technological or sensate triumph. "The dignity of man" is a phrase on the lips of all sorts of people nowadays, including Communist publicists; and by it, all sorts of people mean merely the gratification of the ego, the egalitarian claim that "one man is as good as another, or maybe a little better." Pico, however, knew that no being can dignify himself: dignity is a quality with which one is *invested;* it must be conferred. For human dignity to exist, there must be a Master who can raise Man above the brute creation. If that Master is denied, then dignity for Man is unattainable.

For despite all the cant concerning the dignity of man in our time, the real tendency of recent intellectual currents has been to sweep true human dignity down to a morass of mechanistic indignity. Joseph Wood Krutch, a generation ago, in his *Modern Temper,* described with a sombre resignation this process of degradation. Without God, Man cannot aspire to rank with Cherubim and Seraphim. Freud convinced the crowd of intellectuals that Man was nothing better than the slave of obscure and arrogant fleshly desires; Alfred Kinsey, unintentionally reducing to absurdity this denial of human dignity, advised his fellow-creatures to emulate, if not the ant, at least the snake—for Man, so the modern dogma goes, lives only to lust. In this fashion phrases linger on in men's mouths long after the object they describe has been forgot.

Pico della Mirandola, Platonist and Christian and sorcerer and rhetorician and mystic, designed his nine hundred questions as an irrefragable proof of Man's uniqueness. Emerson echoed him, five centuries after:

> There are two laws discrete
> Not reconciled,—
> Law for man, and law for thing;
> The last builds town and fleet,
> But it runs wild,
> And doth the man unking.

By a discipline of the reason and the will, to make Man kingly, even angelic—this was Pico's hope, and it has been the hope of all true humanists after him. Thing, nevertheless, has run wild in our time, building town and fleet, bomb and satellite; and the Man has been unkinged; and human dignity is at its lowest ebb, now, when Man's power over nature is at its summit. A real man, in any age, is dignified and nobly human in proportion as he acknowledges the overlordship of One greater than Man. If Things are to be thrust out of the saddle once more, and Man mounted (in Pico's phrase) to "join battle as to the sound of a trumpet of war" on behalf of Man's higher nature, then some of us must go barefoot through the world, like Pico, preaching against the vegetative and sensual errors of the time.

RUSSELL KIRK

ORATION ON THE DIGNITY
OF MAN

Most esteemed Fathers, I have read in the ancient writings of the Arabians that Abdala the Saracen[1] on being asked what, on this stage, so to say, of the world, seemed to him most evocative of wonder, replied that there was nothing to be seen more marvelous than man. And that celebrated exclamation of Hermes Trismegistus, "What a great miracle is man, Asclepius"[a] confirms this opinion.

And still, as I reflected upon the basis assigned for these estimations, I was not fully persuaded by the diverse reasons advanced by a variety of persons for the pre-eminence of human nature; for example: that man is the intermediary between creatures, that he is the familiar of the gods above him as he is lord of the beings beneath him; that, by the acuteness of his senses, the inquiry of his reason and the light of his intelligence, he is the interpreter of nature, set midway between the

timeless unchanging and the flux of time;
the living union (as the Persians say), the
very marriage hymn of the world, and, by
David's testimony[3] but little lower than the
angels. These reasons are all, without question, of great weight; nevertheless, they do
not touch the principal reasons, those, that
is to say, which justify man's unique right
to such unbounded admiration. Why, I
asked, should we not admire the angels
themselves and the beatific choirs more?
At long last, however, I feel that I have
come to some understanding of why man
is the most fortunate of living things and,
consequently, deserving of all admiration;
of what may be the condition in the hierarchy of beings assigned to him, which
draws upon him the envy, not of the brutes
alone, but of the astral beings and of the
very intelligences which dwell beyond the
confines of the world. A thing surpassing
belief and smiting the soul with wonder.
Still, how could it be otherwise? For it is
on this ground that man is, with complete
justice, considered and called a great mir-

4

acle and a being worthy of all admiration.

Hear then, oh Fathers, precisely what this condition of man is; and in the name of your humanity, grant me your benign audition as I pursue this theme.

God the Father, the Mightest Architect, had already raised, according to the precepts of His hidden wisdom, this world we see, the cosmic dwelling of divinity, a temple most august. He had already adorned the supercelestial region with Intelligences, infused the heavenly globes with the life of immortal souls and set the fermenting dung-heap of the inferior world teeming with every form of animal life. But when this work was done, the Divine Artificer still longed for some creature which might comprehend the meaning of so vast an achievement, which might be moved with love at its beauty and smitten with awe at its grandeur. When, consequently, all else had been completed (as both Moses and Timaeus testify),[4] in the very last place, He bethought Himself of bringing forth man. Truth was, however, that there remained no archetype according to which He might fashion a new offspring, nor in His treasure-houses the wherewithal to endow a new son with a fitting inheritance, nor any place, among the seats of the universe, where this new creature might dispose himself to contemplate the world. All space was already filled; all things had been distributed in the highest, the middle and the lowest orders. Still, it was not in the nature of the power of the Father to fail in this last creative élan; nor was it in the nature of that supreme Wisdom to hesitate through lack of counsel in so crucial a matter; nor, finally, in the nature of His beneficent love to compel the creature destined to praise the divine generosity in all other things to find it wanting in himself.

At last, the Supreme Maker decreed that this creature, to whom He could give nothing wholly his own, should have a share in the particular endowment of every other creature. Taking man, therefore, this creature of indeterminate image, He set him in the middle of the world and thus spoke to him:

"We have given you, Oh Adam, no visage proper to yourself, nor any endowment properly your own, in order that whatever place, whatever form, whatever gifts you may, with premeditation, select, these same you may have and possess through your own judgment and decision. The nature of all other creatures is defined and restricted within laws which We have laid down; you, by contrast, impeded by no such restrictions, may, by your own free will, to whose custody We have assigned you, trace for yourself the lineaments of your own nature. I have placed you at the very center of the world, so that from that vantage point you may with greater ease glance round about you on all that the world contains. We have made you a creature neither of heaven nor of earth, neither mortal nor immortal, in order that you may, as the free and proud shaper of your own being, fashion yourself in the form you may prefer. It will be in your power to descend to the lower, brutish forms of life; you will be able, through your own decision, to rise again to the superior orders whose life is divine."

Oh unsurpassed generosity of God the Father, Oh wondrous and unsurpassable felicity of man, to whom it is granted to have what he chooses, to be what he wills to be! The brutes, from the moment of their birth, bring with them, as Lucilius says,[5] "from their mother's womb" all that they will ever possess. The highest spiritual beings were, from the very moment of creation, or soon thereafter, fixed in the mode of being which would be theirs through measureless eternities. But upon man, at the moment of his creation, God bestowed seeds pregnant with all possibilities, the germs of every form of life. Whichever of these a man shall cultivate, the same will mature and bear fruit in him. If vegetative, he will become a plant; if sensual, he will become brutish; if rational, he will reveal himself a heavenly being; if intellectual, he will be an angel and the son of God. And if, dissatisfied with the lot of all creatures, he should recollect himself into the center of his own unity, he will there, become one spirit with God, in the solitary darkness of the Father, Who is set above all things, himself transcend all creatures.

Who then will not look with awe upon this our chameleon, or who, at least, will look with greater admiration on any other being? This creature, man, whom Asclepius the Athenian, by reason of this very mutability, this nature capable of transforming itself, quite rightly said was symbolized in the mysteries by the figure of Proteus. This is the source of those metamorphoses, or transformations, so celebrated among the Hebrews and among the Pythagoreans; for even the esoteric theology of the Hebrews at times transforms the holy Enoch into that angel of divinity which is sometimes called *"malakh-ha-shekhinah"* [6] and at other times transforms other personages into divinities of other names;[7] while the Pythagoreans transform men guilty of crimes into brutes or even, if we are to believe Empedocles, into plants; and Mohamet, imitating them, was known frequently to say that the man who deserts the divine law becomes a brute. And he was right; for it is not the bark that makes the tree, but its insensitive and unresponsive nature; nor the hide which makes the beast of burden, but its brute and sensual soul; nor the orbicular form which makes the heavens, but their harmonious order. Finally, it is not freedom from a body, but its spiritual intelligence, which makes the angel. If you see a man dedicated to his stomach, crawling on the ground, you see a plant and not a man; or if you see a man bedazzled by the empty forms of the imagination, as by the wiles of Calypso, and through their alluring solicitations made a slave to his own senses, you see a brute and not a man. If, however, you see a philosopher, judging and distinguishing all things according to the rule of reason, him shall you hold in veneration, for he is a creature of heaven and not of earth; if, finally, a pure contemplator, unmindful of the body, wholly withdrawn into the inner chambers of the mind, here indeed is neither a creature of earth nor a heavenly creature, but some higher divinity, clothed with human flesh.

Who then will not look with wonder upon man, upon man who, not without reason, in the sacred Mosaic and Christian writings, is designated sometimes by the term "all flesh" and sometimes by the term "every creature," because he molds, fashions and transforms himself into the likeness of all flesh and assumes the characteristic power of every form of life? This is why Evantes the Persian[8] in his exposition of the Chaldean theology, writes that man has no inborn and proper semblance, but many which are extraneous and adventitious: whence the Chaldean saying: *"Enosh hu shinnujim vekammah tebhaoth haj"*—"man is a living creature of varied, multiform and ever-changing nature." [9]

But what is the purpose of all this? That we may understand—since we have been born into this condition of being what we choose to be—that we ought to be sure above else that it may never be said against us that, born to a high position, we failed to appreciate it, but fell instead to the estate of brutes and uncomprehending beasts of burden; and that the saying of Asaph the Prophet,[10] "You are all Gods and sons of the Most High," might rather be true; and finally that we may not, through abuse of the generosity of a most indulgent Father, pervert the free option which He has given us from a saving to a damning gift. Let a certain saving ambition invade our souls so that, impatient of mediocrity, we pant after the highest things and (since, if we will, we can) bend all our efforts to their attainment. Let us disdain the things of earth, hold as little worth even the astral orders and, putting behind us all the things of this world, hasten to that court beyond the world, closest to the most exalted Godhead. There, as the sacred mysteries tell us, the Seraphim, Cherubim and Thrones occupy the first places; [11] but, unable to yield to them, and impatient of any second place, let us emulate their dignity and glory. And, if we will it, we shall be inferior to them in nothing.

How must we proceed and what must we do to realize this ambition? Let us observe what they do, what kind of life they lead. For if we lead this kind of life (and we can) we shall attain their same estate. The Seraphim burns with the fire of charity; from the Cherubim flashes forth the splendor of intelligence; the Throne stands firm with the firmness of justice. If, consequently, in the pursuit of the active life we govern inferior things by just criteria, we shall be established in the firm position of the Thrones. If, freeing ourselves from active care, we devote our time to contemplation, meditating upon the Creator in His work, and the work in its Creator, we shall be resplendent with the light of the Cherubim. If we burn with love for the Creator only, His consuming fire will quickly transform us into the flaming likeness of the Seraphim. Above the Throne, that is, above the just judge, God sits, judge of the ages. Above the Cherub, that is, the contemplative spirit, He spreads His wings, nourishing him, as it were, with an enveloping warmth. For the spirit of the Lord moves upon the waters, those waters which are above the heavens and which, according to Job, praise the Lord in pre-aurorial hymns.[12] Whoever is a Seraph, that is a lover, is in God and God is in him; even, it may be said, God and he are one. Great is the power of the Thrones which we attain by right judgment, highest of all the sublimity of the Seraphim which we attain by loving.

But how can anyone judge or love what he does not know? Moses loved the God whom he had seen and as judge of his people he administered what he had previously seen in contemplation on the mountain. Therefore the Cherub is the intermediary and by his light equally prepares us for the fire of the Seraphim and the judgment of the Thrones. This is the bond which unites the highest minds, the Palladian order which presides over contemplative philosophy; this is then the bond which before all else we must emulate, embrace and comprehend, whence we may be rapt to the heights of love or descend, well instructed and prepared, to the duties of the practical life. But certainly it is worth the effort, if we are to form our life on the model of the life of the Cherubim, to have familiarly before our eyes both its nature and its quality as well as the duties and the functions proper to it. Since it is not granted to us, flesh as we are and knowledgeable only of the things of earth, to attain such knowledge by our own efforts, let us have recourse to the ancient Fathers. They can give us the fullest and most reliable testimony concerning these matters because they had an almost domestic and connatural knowledge of them.

Let us ask the Apostle Paul, that vessel of election, in what activity he saw the armies of the Cherubim engaged when he was rapt to the third heaven. He will answer, according to the interpretation of Dionysius, that he saw them first being purified, then illuminated, then finally made perfect. We, therefore, imitating the life of the Cherubim here on earth, by refraining the impulses of our passions through moral science, by dissipating the darkness of reason by dialectic—thus washing away, so to speak, the filth of ignorance and vice —may likewise purify our souls, so that the passions may never run rampant, nor reason, lacking restraint, range beyond its natural limits. Then may we suffuse our purified souls with the light of natural philosophy, bringing it to final perfection by the knowledge of divine things.

Lest we be satisfied to consult only those of our own faith and tradition, let us also have recourse to the patriarch, Jacob, whose likeness, carved on the throne of glory, shines out before us.[13] This wisest of the Fathers who though sleeping in the lower world, still has his eyes fixed on the world above, will admonish us. He will admonish us, however, in a figure, for all things appeared in figures to the men of those times: a ladder rises by many rungs from earth to the height of heaven and at its summit sits the Lord, while over its rungs the contemplative angels move, alternately ascending and descending. If this is what we, who wish to imitate the angelic life, must do in our turn, who, I ask, would dare set muddied feet or soiled hands to the ladder of the Lord? It is forbidden, as the mysteries teach, for the impure to touch what is pure. But what are these hands, these feet, of which we speak? The feet, to be sure, of the soul: that is, its most despicable portion by which the soul is held fast to earth as a root to the ground; I mean to say, its alimentary and nutritive faculty where lust ferments and voluptuous softness is fostered. And why may we not call "the hand" that irascible power of the soul, which is the warrior of the appetitive faculty, fighting for it and foraging for it in the dust and the sun, seizing for it all the things which, sleeping in the shade, it will devour? Let us bathe in moral philosophy as in a living stream, these hands, that is, the whole sensual part in which the lusts of the body have their seat and which, as the saying is, holds the soul by the scruff of the neck, lest we be flung back from that ladder as profane and polluted intruders. Even this, however, will not be enough, if we wish to be the companions of the angels who traverse the ladder of Jacob, unless we are first instructed and rendered able to advance on that ladder duely, step by step, at no point to stray from it and to complete the alternate ascensions and descents. When we shall have been so prepared by the art of discourse or of reason, then, inspired by the spirit of the Cherubim, exercising philosophy through all the rungs of the ladder —that is, of nature—we shall penetrate being from its center to its surface and from its surface to its center. At one time we shall descend, dismembering with titanic force the "unity" of the "many," like the members of Osiris; at another time we shall ascend, recollecting those same members, by the power of Phoebus, into their original unity. Finally, in the bosom of the Father, who reigns above the ladder, we shall find perfection and peace in the felicity of theological knowledge.

Let us also inquire of the just Job, who made his covenant with the God of life even before he entered into life, what, above all else, the supreme God desires of those tens of thousands of beings which surround Him. He will answer, without a doubt: peace, just as it is written in the pages of Job: He establishes peace in the high reaches of heaven.[14] And since the middle order interprets the admonitions of the higher to the lower orders, the words of Job the theologian may well be interpreted for us by Empedocles the philosopher.[15] Empedocles teaches us that there is in our souls a dual nature; the one bears us upward toward the heavenly regions; by the other we are dragged downward toward regions infernal, through friendship and discord, war and peace; so witness those verses in which he laments that, torn by strife and discord, like a madman, in flight from the gods, he is driven into the depths of the sea. For it is a patent thing, oh Fathers, that many forces strive within us, in grave, intestine warfare, worse than the civil wars of states. Equally clear is it that, if we are to overcome this warfare, if we are to achieve that peace which must establish us finally among the exalted of God, philosophy alone can compose and allay that strife. In the first place, if our man seeks only truce with his enemies, moral philosophy will restrain the unreasoning drives of the protean brute, the passionate violence and wrath of the lion within us. If, acting on wiser counsel, we should seek to secure an unbroken peace, moral philosophy will still be at hand to fulfill our desires abundantly; and having slain either beast, like sacrificed sows, it will establish an inviolable compact of peace between the flesh and the spirit. Dialectic will compose the disorders of reason torn by anxiety and uncertainty amid the conflicting hordes of words and captious reasonings. Natural philosophy will reduce the conflict of opinions and the endless debates which from every side vex, distract and lacerate the disturbed mind. It will compose this conflict, however, in such a manner as to remind us that nature, as Heraclitus wrote, is generated by war and for this reason is called by Homer, "strife." Natural philosophy, therefore, cannot assure us a true and unshakable peace. To bestow such peace is rather the privilege and office of the queen of the sciences, most holy theology. Natural philosophy will at best point out the way to theology and even accompany us along the path, while theology, seeing us from afar hastening to draw close to her, will call out: "Come to me you who are spent in labor and I will restore you; come to me and I will give you the peace which the world and nature cannot give." [16]

Summoned in such consoling tones and invited with such kindness, like earthly Mercuries, we shall fly on winged feet to embrace that most blessed mother and there enjoy the peace we have longed for: that most holy peace, that indivisible union, that seamless friendship through which all souls will not only be at one in that one mind which is above every mind, but, in a manner which passes expression, will really be one, in the most profound depths of being. This is the friendship which the Pythagoreans say is the purpose of all philosophy. This is the peace which God established in the high places of the heaven and which the angels, descending to earth, announced to men of good will, so that men, ascending through this peace to heaven, might become angels. This is the peace which we would wish for our friends, for our age, for every house into which we enter and for our own soul, that through this peace it may become the dwelling of God; so that, too, when the soul, by means of moral philosophy and dialectic shall have purged herself of her uncleanness, adorned herself with the many disciplines of philosophy as

with the raiment of a prince's court and
crowned the pediments of her doors with
the garlands of theology, the King of Glory
may descend and, coming with the Father,
take up his abode with her. If she prove
worthy of so great a guest, she will, through
his boundless clemency, arrayed in the
golden vesture of the many sciences as in
a nuptial gown, receive him, not as a guest
merely, but as a spouse. And rather than
be parted from him, she will prefer to leave
her own people and her father's house.
Forgetful of her very self she will desire to
die to herself in order to live in her spouse,
in whose eyes the death of his saints is
infinitely precious: I mean that death—if
the very plenitude of life can be called
death—whose meditation wise men have
always held to be the special study of
philosophy.[17]

Let us also cite Moses himself, who is
but little removed from the living well-
spring of the most holy and ineffable understanding by whose nectar the angels are
inebriated. Let us listen to the venerable

judge as he enunciates his laws to us who live in the desert solitude of the body: "Let those who, still unclean, have need of moral philosophy, dwell with the peoples outside the tabernacle, under the open sky, until, like the priests of Thessaly, they shall have cleansed themselves. Those who have already brought order into their own lives may be received into the tabernacle, but still may not touch the sacred vessels. Let them rather first, as zealous levites, in the service of dialectic, minister to the holy offices of philosophy. When they shall themselves be admitted to those offices, they may, as priests of philosophy, contemplate the many-colored throne of the higher God, that is the courtly palace of the star-hung heavens, the heavenly candelabrum aflame with seven lights and the elements which are the furry veils of his tabernacle;[18] so that, finally, having been permitted to enter, through the merit of sublime theology, into the innermost chambers of the temple, with no veil of images interposing itself, we may enjoy the glory

of divinity." This is what Moses beyond a
doubt commands us, admonishing, urging
and exhorting us to prepare for ourselves,
while we may, by means of philosophy, a
road to future heavenly glory.

In fact, however, the dignity of the liberal arts, which I am about to discuss, and
their value to us is attested not only by
the Mosaic and Christian mysteries but
also by the theologies of the most ancient
times. What else is to be understood by
the stages through which the initiates must
pass in the mysteries of the Greeks? These
initiates, after being purified by the arts
which we might call expiatory, moral philosophy and dialectic, were granted admission to the mysteries. What could such
admission mean but the interpretation of
occult nature by means of philosophy?
Only after they had been prepared in this
way did they receive "*Epopteia*," that is,
the immediate vision of divine things by
the light of theology. Who would not long
to be admitted to such mysteries? Who
would not desire, putting all human con-

cerns behind him, holding the goods of
fortune in contempt and little minding the
goods of the body, thus to become, while
still a denizen of earth, a guest at the table
of the gods, and, drunk with the nectar of
eternity, receive, while still a mortal, the
gift of immortality? Who would not wish
to be so inspired by those Socratic frenzies
which Plato sings in the *Phaedrus*[19] that,
swiftly fleeing this place, that is, this world
fixed in evil, by the oars, so to say, both of
feet and wings, he might reach the heavenly Jerusalem by the swiftest course? Let
us be driven, Oh Fathers, by those Socratic
frenzies which lift us to such ecstasy that
our intellects and our very selves are united
to God. And we shall be moved by them
in this way if previously we have done all
that it lies in us to do. If, by moral philosophy, the power of our passions shall have
been restrained by proper controls so that
they achieve harmonious accord; and if, by
dialectic, our reason shall have progressed
by an ordered advance, then, smitten by
the frenzy of the Muses, we shall hear the

heavenly harmony with the inward ears of the spirit. Then the leader of the Muses, Bacchus, revealing to us in our moments of philosophy, through his mysteries, that is, the visible signs of nature, the invisible things of God,[20] will make us drunk with the richness of the house of God; and there, if, like Moses, we shall prove entirely faithful, most sacred theology will supervene to inspire us with redoubled ecstasy. For, raised to the most eminent height of theology, whence we shall be able to measure with the rod of indivisible eternity all things that are and that have been; and, grasping the primordial beauty of things, like the seers of Phoebus, we shall become the winged lovers of theology. And at last, smitten by the ineffable love as by a sting, and, like the Seraphim, born outside ourselves, filled with the godhead, we shall be, no longer ourselves, but the very One who made us.

The sacred names of Apollo, to anyone who penetrates their meanings and the mysteries they conceal, clearly show that

God is a philosopher no less than a seer; but since Ammonius has amply treated this theme, there is no occasion for me to expound it anew. Nevertheless, Oh Fathers, we cannot fail to recall those three Delphic precepts which are so very necessary for everyone about to enter the most holy and august temple, not of the false, but of the true Apollo who illumines every soul as it enters this world.[21] You will see that they exhort us to nothing else but to embrace with all our powers this tripartite philosophy which we are now discussing. As a matter of fact that aphorism: μηδὲν ἄγαν, that is: "Nothing too much," duly prescribes a measure and rule for all the virtues through the concept of the "Mean" of which moral philosophy treats. In like manner, that other aphorism γνῶθι οεαυτὸν, that is, "Know thyself," invites and exhorts us to the study of the whole nature of which the nature of man is the connecting link and the "mixed potion"; for he who knows himself knows all things in himself, as Zoroaster first and after him Plato, in the

Alcibiades, wrote.[22] Finally, enlightened by this knowledge, through the aid of natural philosophy, being already close to God, employing the theological salutation $εἶ$, that is "Thou art," we shall blissfully address the true Apollo on intimate terms.

Let us also seek the opinion of Pythagoras, that wisest of men, known as a wise man precisely because he never thought himself worthy of that name. His first precept to us will be: "Never to sit on a bushel"; never, that is, through slothful inaction to lose our power of reason, that faculty by which the mind examines, judges and measures all things; but rather unremittingly by the rule and exercise of dialectic, to direct it and keep it agile. Next he will warn us of two things to be avoided at all costs: Neither to make water facing the sun, nor to cut our nails while offering sacrifice. Only when, by moral philosophy, we shall have evacuated the weakening appetites of our too-abundant pleasures and pared away, like nail clippings, the sharp points of anger and wrath in our souls, shall we finally begin to take part in the sacred rites, that is, the mysteries of Bacchus of which we have spoken and to dedicate ourselves to that contemplation of which the Sun is rightly called the father and the guide. Finally, Pythagoras will command us to "Feed the cock"; that is, to nourish the divine part of our soul with the knowledge of divine things as with substantial food and heavenly ambrosia. This is the cock whose visage the lion, that is, all earthly power, holds in fear and awe. This is the cock to whom, as we read in Job, understanding was given. At this cock's crowing, erring man returns to his senses. This is the cock which every day, in the morning twilight, with the stars of morning, raises a *Te Deum* to heaven. This is the cock which Socrates, at the hour of his death, when he hoped that he was about to join the divinity of his spirit to the divinity of the higher world and when he was already beyond danger of any bodily illness, said that he owed to Asclepius, that is, the healer of souls.[23]

Let us also pass in review the records of the Chaldeans; there we shall see (if they are to be believed) that the road to happiness, for mortals, lies through these same arts. The Chaldean interpreters write that it was a saying of Zoroaster that the soul is a winged creature. When her wings fall from her, she is plunged into the body; but when they grow strong again, she flies back to the supernal regions. And when his disciples asked him how they might insure that their souls might be well plumed and hence swift in flight he replied: "Water them well with the waters of life." And when they persisted, asking whence they might obtain these waters of life, he answered (as he was wont) in a parable: "The Paradise of God is bathed and watered by four rivers; from these same sources you may draw the waters which will save you. The name of the river which flows from the north is Pischon which means, "the Right." That which flows from the west is Gichon, that is, "Expiation." The river flowing from the east is named

Chiddekel, that is, "Light," while that, finally, from the south is Perath, which may be understood as "Compassion." Consider carefully and with full attention, Oh Fathers, what these deliverances of Zoroaster might mean. Obviously, they can only mean that we should, by moral science, as by western waves, wash the uncleanness from our eyes; that, by dialectic, as by a reading taken by the northern star, our gaze must be aligned with the right. Then, that we should become accustomed to bear, in the contemplation of nature, the still feeble light of truth, like the first rays of the rising sun, so that finally we may, through theological piety and the most holy cult of God, become able, like the eagles of heaven, to bear the effulgent splendor of the noonday sun. These are, perhaps, those "morning, midday and evening thoughts" which David first celebrated and on which St. Augustine later expatiated.[24] This is the noonday light which inflames the Seraphim toward their goal and equally illuminates the Cherubim.

This is the promised land toward which our ancient father Abraham was ever advancing; this the region where, as the teachings of the Cabalists and the Moors tell us, there is no place for unclean spirits. And if we may be permitted, even in the form of a riddle, to say anything publicly about the deeper mysteries: since the precipitous fall of man from heaven has left his mind in a vertiginous whirl and since according to Jeremiah,[25] death has come in through the windows to infect our hearts and bowels with evil, let us call upon Raphael, the heavenly healer that by moral philosophy and dialectic, as with healing drugs, he may release us. When we shall have been restored to health, Gabriel, the strength of God, will abide in us. Leading us through the marvels of nature and pointing out to us everywhere the power and the goodness of God, he will deliver us finally to the care of the High Priest Michael. He, in turn, will adorn those who have successfully completed their service to philosophy with the priesthood of theology as with a crown of precious stones.

These are the reasons, most reverend Fathers, which not only led, but even compelled me, to the study of philosophy. And I should not have undertaken to expound them, except to reply to those who are wont to condemn the study of philosophy, especially among men of high rank, but also among those of modest station. For the whole study of philosophy (such is the unhappy plight of our time) is occasion for contempt and contumely, rather than honor and glory. The deadly and monstrous persuasion has invaded practically all minds, that philosophy ought not to be studied at all or by very few people; as though it were a thing of little worth to have before our eyes and at our finger-tips, as matters we have searched out with greatest care, the causes of things, the ways of nature and the plan of the universe, God's counsels and the mysteries of heaven and of earth, unless by such knowledge one might procure some profit or favor for oneself. Thus we have reached the point, it is painful to recognize, where the only persons accounted wise are those who can reduce the pursuit of wisdom to a profitable traffic; and chaste Pallas, who dwells among men only by the generosity of the gods, is rejected, hooted, whistled at in scorn, with no one to love or befriend her unless, by prostituting herself, she is able to pay back into the strongbox of her lover the ill-procured price of her deflowered virginity. I address all these complaints, with the greatest regret and indignation, not against the princes of our times, but against the philosophers who believe and assert that philosophy should not be pursued because no monetary value or reward is assigned it, unmindful that by this sign they disqualify themselves as philosophers. Since their whole life is concentrated on gain and ambition, they never embrace the knowledge of the truth for its own sake. This much will I say for myself—and on this point I do not blush for praising myself—that I have never philosophized save for the sake of philosophy, nor have I ever desired or hoped to secure from my studies and my laborious researches any profit or fruit save cultivation of mind and knowledge of the truth—things I esteem more and more with the passage of time. I have also been so avid for this knowledge and so enamoured of it that I have set aside all private and public concerns to devote myself completely to contemplation; and from it no calumny of jealous persons, nor any invective from the enemies of wisdom has ever been nor ever will be able to detach me. Philosophy has taught me to rely on my own convictions rather than on the judgments of others and to concern myself less with whether I am well thought of than whether what I do or say is evil.

I was not unaware, most revered Fathers, that this present disputation of mine would be as acceptable and as pleasing to you, who favor all the good arts and who have consented to grace it with your presence, as it would be irritating and offensive to many others. I am also aware that there is no dearth of those who have condemned

my undertaking before this and continue
to do so on a number of grounds. But this
has always been the case: works which are
well-intentioned and sincerely directed to
virtue have always had no fewer—not to
say more—detractors than those undertaken for questionable motives and for
devious ends. Some persons disapprove the
present type of disputation in general and
this method of disputing in public about
learned matters; they assert that they serve
only the exhibition of talent and display
of opinion, rather than the increase of
learning. Others do not disapprove this
type of exercise, but resent the fact that
at my age, a mere twenty-four years, I have
dared to propose a disputation concerning
the most subtle mysteries of Christian theology, the most debated points of philosophy and unfamiliar branches of learning;
and that I have done so here, in this most
renowned of cities, before a large assembly
of very learned men, in the presence of
the Apostolic Senate. Still others have conceded my right so to dispute, but have not

conceded that I might dispute nine hundred theses, asserting that such a project is superfluous, over-ambitious and beyond my powers. I should have acceded to these objections willingly and immediately, if the philosophy which I profess had so counseled me. Nor should I now undertake to reply to them, as my philosophy urges me to do, if I believed that this disputation between us were undertaken for purposes of mere altercation and litigation. Therefore, let all intention of denigration and exasperation be purged from our minds and with it that malice which, as Plato writes, is never present in the angelic choirs. Let us amicably decide whether it be admissible for me to proceed with my disputation and whether I should venture so large a number of questions.

I shall not, in the first place, have much to say against those who disapprove this type of public disputation. It is a crime— if it be a crime—which I share with all of you, most excellent doctors, who have engaged in such exercises on many occasions to the enhancement of your reputations, as well as with Plato and Aristotle and all the most esteemed philosophers of every age. These philosophers of the past all thought that nothing could profit them more in their search for wisdom than frequent participation in public disputation. Just as the powers of the body are made stronger through gymnastic, the powers of the mind grow in strength and vigor in this arena of learning. I am inclined to believe that the poets, when they sang of the arms of Pallas and the Hebrews, when they called the *"barzel,"* that is, the sword,[26] the symbol of men of wisdom, could have meant nothing by these symbols but this type of contest, at once so necessary and so honorable for the acquisition of knowledge. This may also be the reason why the Chaldeans, at the birth of a man destined to be a philosopher, described a horoscope in which Mars confronted Mercury from three distinct angles. This is as much as to say that should these assemblies and these contests be abandoned, all philosophy would become sluggish and dormant.

It is more difficult for me, however, to find a line of defense against those who tell me that I am unequal to the undertaking. If I say that I *am* equal to it, I shall appear to entertain an immodestly high opinion of myself. If I admit that I am unequal to it, while persisting in it, I shall certainly risk being called temerarious and imprudent. You see the difficulties into which I have fallen, the position in which I am placed. I cannot, without censure, promise something about myself, nor, without equal censure, fail in what I promise. Perhaps I can invoke that saying of Job: "The spirit is in all men." [27] or take consolation in what was said to Timothy: "Let no man despise your youth." [28] But to speak from my own conscience, I might say with greater truth that there is nothing singular about me. I admit that I am devoted to study and eager in the pursuit of the good arts. Nevertheless, I do not assume nor arrogate to myself the title learned. If, consequently, I have taken such a great burden on my shoulders, it is not because I am ignorant of my own weaknesses. Rather, it is because I understand that in this kind of learned contest the real victory lies in being vanquished. Even the weakest, consequently, ought not to shun them, but should seek them out, as well they may. For the one who is bested receives from his conqueror, not an injury but a benefit; he returns to his house richer than he left, that is, more learned and better armed for future contests. Inspired by such hope, though myself but a weak soldier, I have not been afraid to enter so dangerous a contest even against the very strongest and vigorous opponents. Whether, in doing so, I have acted foolishly or not might better be judged from the outcome of the contest than from my age.

I must, in the third place, answer those who are scandalized by the large number of propositions and the variety of topics I have proposed for disputation, as though the burden, however great it may be, rested on their shoulders and not, as it does, on mine. Surely it is unbecoming and captious to want to set limits to another's efforts and, as Cicero says,[29] to desire mediocrity in those things in which the rule should be: the more the better. In undertaking so great a venture only one alternative confronted me: success or failure. If I should succeed, I do not see how it would be more praiseworthy to succeed in defending ten theses than in defending nine hundred. If I should fail, those who hate me will have grounds for disparagement, while those who love me will have an occasion to excuse me. In so large and important an undertaking it would seem that a young man who fails through weakness of talent or want of learning deserves indulgence rather than censure. For as the poet[30] says,

> if powers fail, there shall be praise for daring; and in great undertaking, to have willed is enough

In our own day, many scholars, imitating Gorgias of Leontini, have been accustomed to dispute, not nine hundred questions merely, but the whole range of questions concerning all the arts and have been praised for it. Why should not I, then, without incurring criticism, be permitted to discuss a large number of questions indeed, but questions which are clear and determined in their scope? They reply, this is superfluous and ambitious. I protest that, in my case, no superfluity is involved, but that all is necessary. If they consider the method of my philosophy they will feel compelled, even against their inclinations, to recognize this necessity. All those who attach themselves to one or another of the philosophers, to Thomas, for instance, or Scotus, who at present enjoy the widest following, can indeed test their doctrine in a discussion of a few questions. By contrast, I have so trained myself that, committed to the teachings of no one man, I have ranged through all the masters of philosophy, examined all their works, become acquainted with all schools. As a consequence, I have had to introduce all of them into the discussion lest, defending a doctrine peculiar to one, I might seem committed to it and thus to deprecate the rest. While a few of the theses proposed concern individual philosophers, it was inevitable that a great number should concern all of them together. Nor should anyone condemn me on the grounds that "wherever the storm blows me, there I remain as a guest."[31] For it was a rule among the ancients, in the case of all writers, never to leave unread any commentaries which might be available. Aristotle especially observed this rule so carefully that Plato called him: ἀναγνωσίης, that is, "the reader." It is certainly a mark of excessive narrowness of mind to enclose oneself within one Porch or Academy; nor can anyone reasonably attach himself to one school or philosopher, unless he has previously become familiar with them all. In addition, there is in each school some distinctive characteristic which it does not share with any other.

To begin with the men of our own faith[32] to whom philosophy came last, there is in

John Scotus both vigor and distinction, in Thomas, solidity and sense of balance, in Egidius, lucidity and precision, in Francis, depth and acuteness, in Albert, a sense for ultimate issues, all-embracing and grand, in Henry, as it has seemed to me, always an element of sublimity which inspires reverence. Among the Arabians, there is in Averroës something solid and unshaken, in Avempace, as in Al-Farabi, something serious and deeply meditated; in Avicenna, something divine and platonic. Among the Greeks philosophy was always brilliant and, among the earliest, even chaste: in Simplicius it is rich and abundant, in Themistius elegant and compendious, in Alexander, learned and self-consistent, in Theophrastes, worked out with great reflection, in Ammonius, smooth and pleasing. If you turn to the Platonists, to mention but a few, you will, in Porphyry, be delighted by the wealth of matter and by his preoccupation with many aspects of religion; in Iamblicus, you will be awed by his knowledge of occult philosophy and

45

the mysteries of the barbarian peoples; in
Plotinus, you will find it impossible to
single out one thing for admiration, because he is admirable under every aspect.
Platonists themselves, sweating over his
pages, understand him only with the greatest difficulty when, in his oblique style, he
teaches divinely about divine things and
far more than humanly about things human. I shall pass over the more recent
figures, Proclus, and those others who derive from him, Damacius, Olympiodorus
and many more in whom that τὸ θεῖον, that
is, that divine something which is the special mark of the Platonists, always shines
out.

It should be added that any school which
attacks the more established truths and
by clever slander ridicules the valid arguments of reason confirms, rather than
weakens, the truth itself, which, like em-
bers, is fanned to life, rather than extin-
guished by stirring. These considerations
have motivated me in my determination to
bring to men's attention the opinions of all

schools rather than the doctrine of some
one or other (as some might have pre-
ferred), for it seems to me that by the
confrontation of many schools and the discussion of many philosophical systems that
"effulgence of truth" of which Plato writes
in his letters[33] might illuminate our minds
more clearly, like the sun rising from the
sea. What should have been our plight had
only the philosophical thought of the Latin
authors, that is, Albert, Thomas, Scotus,
Egidius, Francis and Henry, been discussed, while that of the Greeks and the
Arabs was passed over, since all the
thought of the barbarian nations was in-
herited by the Greeks and from the Greeks
came down to us? For this reason, our
thinkers have always been satisfied, in the
field of philosophy, to rest on the discoveries of foreigners and simply to perfect
the work of others. What profit would have
derived from discussing natural philosophy with the Peripatetics, if the Academy
of the Platonists had not also participated
in the exchange, for the doctrine of the

47

latter, even when it touched on divine matters, has always (as St. Augustine bears witness) been esteemed the most elevated of all philosophies? And this in turn has been the reason why I have, for the first time after many centuries of neglect (and there is nothing invidious in my saying so) brought it forth again for public examination and discussion. And what would it have profited us if, having discussed the opinions of innumerable others, like *"asymboli"* [34] at the banquet of wise men, we should contribute nothing of our own, nothing conceived and elaborated by our own mind? Indeed, it is the characteristic of the impotent (as Seneca writes) [35] to have their knowledge all written down in note-books, as though the discoveries of those who preceded us had closed the path to our own efforts, as though the power of nature had become effete in us and could bring forth nothing which, if it could not demonstrate the truth, might at least point to it from afar. The farmer hates sterility in his field and the husband deplores it in his wife; even more then must the divine mind hate the sterile mind with which it is joined and associated, because it hopes from that source to have offspring of such a higher nature.

For these reasons, I have not been content to repeat well-worn doctrines, but have proposed for disputation many points of the early theology of Hermes Trismegistus, many theses drawn from the teachings of the Chaldeans and the Pythagoreans, from the occult mysteries of the Hebrews and, finally, a considerable number of propositions concerning both nature and God which we ourselves have discovered and worked out. In the first place, we have proposed a harmony between Plato and Aristotle, such as many have before this time indeed believed to exist but which no one has satisfactorily established. Boethius, among Latin writers, promised to compose such a harmony, but he never carried his proposal to completion. St. Augustine also writes, in his *Contra Academicos*,[36] that many others tried to prove the same thing,

that is, that the philosophies of Plato and
Aristotle were identical, and by the most
subtle arguments. For example, John the
Grammarian held that Aristotle differed
from Plato only for those who did not
grasp Plato's thought; but he left it to posterity to prove it. We have, in addition, adduced a great number of passages in which
Scotus and Thomas, and others in which
Averroës and Avicenna, have heretofore
been thought to disagree, but which I assert are in harmony with one another.

In the second place, along with my own
reflections on and developments of both
the Aristotelian and the Platonic philosophies, I have adduced seventy-two theses
in physics and metaphysics. If I am not
mistaken (and this will become clearer in
the course of the proposed disputation)
anyone subscribing to these theses will be
able to resolve any question proposed to
him in natural philosophy or theology on a
principle quite other than that taught us
in the philosophy which is at present to be
learned in the schools and is taught by the

masters of the present generation. Nor ought anyone to be surprised, that in my early years, at a tender age at which I should hardly be permitted to read the writings of others (as some have insinuated) I should wish to propose a new philosophy. They ought rather to praise this new philosophy, if it is well defended, or reject it, if it is refuted. Finally, since it will be their task to judge my discoveries and my scholarship, they ought to look to the merit or demerit of these and not to the age of their author.

I have, in addition, introduced a new method of philosophizing on the basis of numbers. This method is, in fact, very old, for it was cultivated by the ancient theologians, by Pythagoras, in the first place, but also by Aglaophamos, Philolaus and Plato, as well as by the earliest Platonists; however, like other illustrious achievements of the past, it has through lack of interest on the part of succeeding generations, fallen into such desuetude, that hardly any vestiges of it are to be found. Plato writes in the *Epinomis*[37] that among all the liberal arts and contemplative sciences, the science of numbering is supreme and most divine. And in another place, asking why man is the wisest of animals, he replies, because he knows how to count. Similarly, Aristotle, in his *Problems*[38] repeats this opinion. Abumasar writes that it was a favorite saying of Avenzoar of Babylon that the man who knows how to count, knows everything else as well. These opinions are certainly devoid of any truth if by the art of number they intend that art in which today merchants excel all other men; Plato adds his testimony to this view, admonishing us emphatically not to confuse this divine arithmetic with the arithmetic of the merchants.[39] When, consequently, after long nights of study I seemed to myself to have thoroughly penetrated this Arithmetic, which is thus so highly extolled, I promised myself that in order to test the matter, I would try to solve by means of this method of number seventy-four questions which are considered, by common consent, among the most important in physics and divinity.

I have also proposed certain theses concerning magic, in which I have indicated that magic has two forms. One consists wholly in the operations and powers of demons, and this consequently appears to me, as God is my witness, an execrable and monstrous thing. The other proves, when thoroughly investigated, to be nothing else but the highest realization of natural philosophy. The Greeks noted both these forms. However, because they considered the first form wholly undeserving the name magic they called it γοητεία, reserving the term μαγεία, to the second, and understanding by it the highest and most perfect wisdom. The term "magus" in the Persian tongue, according to Porphyry, means the same as "interpreter" and "worshiper of the divine" in our language. Moreover, Fathers, the disparity and dissimilarity between these arts is the greatest that can be imagined. Not the Christian religion alone, but all legal codes and every well-governed commonwealth execrates and condemns the first; the second, by contrast, is approved and embraced by all wise men and by all peoples solicitous of heavenly and divine things. The first is the most deceitful of arts; the second, a higher and holier philosophy. The former is vain and disappointing; the latter, firm, solid and satisfying. The practitioner of the first always tries to conceal his addiction, because it always redounds to shame and reproach, while the cultivation of the second, both in antiquity and at almost all periods, has been the source of the highest renown and glory in the field of learning. No philosopher of any worth, eager in pursuit of the good arts, was ever a student of the former, but to learn the latter, Pythagoras, Empedocles, Plato and Democritus crossed the seas. Returning to their homes, they, in turn, taught it to others and considered it a treasure to be closely guarded. The former, since it is supported by no true arguments, is defended by no writers of reputation; the latter, honored, as it were, in its illustrious progenitors, counts two principal authors: Zamolxis, who was imitated by Abaris the Hyperborean, and Zoroaster; not, indeed, the Zoroaster who may immediately come to your minds, but that other Zoroaster, the son of Oromasius. It we should ask Plato the nature of each of these forms of magic, he will respond in the *Alcibiades*[40] that the magic of Zoroaster is nothing else than that science of divine things in which the kings of the Persians had their sons educated to that they might learn to rule their commonwealth on the pattern of the commonwealth of the universe. In the *Charmides*[41] he will answer that the magic of Zamolxis is the medicine of the soul, because it brings temperance to the soul as medicine brings health to the body. Later Charondas, Damigeron, Apollonius, Osthanes and Dardanus continued in their footsteps, as did Homer, of whom we shall sometime prove, in a "poetic theology" we propose to write, that he concealed this doctrine, symbolically, in the wanderings of his

55

Ulysses, just as he did all other learned doctrines. They were also followed by Eudoxus and Hermippus, as well as by practically all those who studied the Pythagorean and Platonic mysteries. Of later philosophers, I find that three had ferreted it out: the Arabian, Al-Kindi, Roger Bacon and William of Paris.[42] Plotinus also gives signs that he was aware of it in the passage in which he shows that the magician is the minister of nature and not merely its artful imitator. This very wise man approves and maintains this magic, while so abhorring that other that once, when he was invited to take part in rites of evil spirits, he said that they ought rather to come to him, than he go to them; and he spoke well. Just as that first form of magic makes man a slave and pawn of evil powers, the latter makes him their lord and master. That first form of magic cannot justify any claim to being either an art or a science while the latter, filled as it is with mysteries, embraces the most profound contemplation of the deepest secrets of things and finally the knowl-

edge of the whole of nature. This beneficent magic, in calling forth, as it were,
from their hiding places into the light the
powers which the largess of God has sown
and planted in the world, does not itself
work miracles, so much as sedulously serve
nature as she works her wonders. Scru-
tinizing, with greater penetration, that
harmony of the universe which the
Greeks with greater aptness of terms
called συμπάθεια and grasping the mutual
affinity of things, she applies to each thing
those inducements (called the ἴυγγες of the
magicians), most suited to its nature. Thus
it draws forth into public notice the miracles which lie hidden in the recesses of
the world, in the womb of nature, in the
storehouses and secret vaults of God,
as though she herself were their artificer.
As the farmer weds his elms to the vines,
so the "magus" unites earth to heaven, that
is, the lower orders to the endowments and
the powers of the higher. Hence it is that
this latter magic appears the more divine
and salutary, as the former presents a

monstrous and destructive visage. But the deepest reason for the difference is the fact that that first magic, delivering man over to the enemies of God, alienates him from God, while the second, beneficent magic, excites in him an admiration for the works of God which flowers naturally into charity, faith and hope. For nothing so surely impels us to the worship of God than the assiduous contemplation of His miracles and when, by means of this natural magic, we shall have examined these wonders more deeply, we shall more ardently be moved to love and worship Him in his works, until finally we shall be compelled to burst into the song: "The heavens, all of the earth, is filled with the majesty of your glory." But enough about magic. I have been led to say even this much because I know that there are many persons who condemn it and hate it, because they do not understand it, just as dogs always bay at strangers.

I come now to those matters which I have drawn from the ancient mysteries of

the Hebrews and here adduce in confirmation of the inviolable Catholic faith. Lest
these matters be thought, by those to
whom they are unfamiliar, bubbles of the
imaginations and tales of charlatans, I want
everyone to understand what they are and
what their true character is; whence they
are drawn and who are the illustrious writers who testify to them; how mysterious
they are, and divine and necessary to men
of our faith for the propagation of our religion in the face of the persistent calumnies
of the Hebrews. Not famous Hebrew
teachers alone, but, from among those of
our own persuasion, Esdras, Hilary and
Origen[43] all write that Moses, in addition
to the law of the five books which he
handed down to posterity, when on the
mount, received from God a more secret
and true explanation of the law. They also
say that God commanded Moses to make
the law known to the people, but not to
write down its interpretation or to divulge
it, but to communicate it only to Jesu
Nave[44] who, in turn, was to reveal it to

59

succeeding high priests under a strict obligation of silence. It was enough to indicate, through simple historical narrative, the power of God, his wrath against the unjust, his mercy toward the good, his justice toward all and to educate the people, by divine and salutary commands, to live well and blessedly and to worship in the true religion. Openly to reveal to the people the hidden mysteries and the secret intentions of the highest divinity, which lay concealed under the hard shell of the law and the rough vesture of language, what else could this be but to throw holy things to dogs and to strew gems among swine? The decision, consequently, to keep such things hidden from the vulgar and to communicate them only to the initiate, among whom alone, as Paul says, wisdom speaks, was not a counsel of human prudence but a divine command. And the philosophers of antiquity scrupulously observed this caution. Pythagoras wrote nothing but a few trifles which he confided to his daughter Dama, on his deathbed. The Sphinxes, which are carved on the temples of the Egyptians, warned that the mystic doctrines be kept inviolate from the profane multitude by means of riddles. Plato, writing certain things to Dionysius concerning the highest substances, explained that he had to write in riddles "lest the letter fall into other hands and others come to know the things I have intended for you." Aristotle used to say that the books of the *Metaphysics* in which he treats of divine matters were both published and unpublished. Is there any need for further instances? Origen asserts that Jesus Christ, the Teacher of Life, revealed many things to His disciples which they in turn were unwilling to commit to writing lest they become the common possession of the crowd. Dionysius the Areopagite gives powerful confirmation to this assertion when he writes that the more secret mysteries were transmitted by the founders of our religion ἐκ νου εἰς νουν διὰ μέσον λόγου, that is, from mind to mind, without commitment to writing, through the medium

61

of the spoken word alone. Because the true interpretation of the law given to Moses was, by God's command, revealed in almost precisely this same way, it was called "Cabala," which in Hebrew means the same as our word "reception." The precise point is, of course, that that doctrine was received by one man from another not through written documents but, as a hereditary right, through a regular succession of revelations.

After Cyrus had delivered the Hebrews from the Babylonian captivity, and the Temple had been restored under Zorobabel, the Hebrews bethought themselves of restoring the law. Esdras, who was head of the church at the time, amended the book of Moses. He readily realized, moreover, that because of the exiles, the massacres, the flights and the captivity of the people of Israel, the practice established by the ancients of handing down the doctrines by word of mouth could not be maintained. Unless they were committed to writing, the heavenly teachings divinely handed down must inevitably perish, for the memory of them would not long endure. He decided, consequently, that all of the wise men still alive should be convened and that each should communicate to the convention all that he remembered about the mysteries of the law. Their communications were then to be collected by scribes into seventy volumes (approximately the same number as there were members of the Sanhedrin). So that you need not accept my testimony alone, Oh Fathers, hear Esdras himself speaking: "After forty days had passed, the All-Highest spoke and said: The first things which you wrote publish openly so that the worthy and the unworthy alike may read; but the last seventy books conserve so that you may hand them on to the wise men among your people, for in these reside the spring of understanding, the fountain of wisdom and the river of knowledge. And I did these things." [45] These are the very words of Esdras. These are the books of cabalistic wisdom. In these books, as Esdras unmistakably states, resides the springs of understanding, that is, the ineffable theology of the supersubstantial deity; the fountain of wisdom, that is, the precise metaphysical doctrine concerning intelligible and angelic forms; and the stream of wisdom, that is, the best established philosophy concerning nature. Pope Sixtus the Fourth, the immediate predecessor of our present pope, Innocent the Eighth, under whose happy reign we are living, took all possible measures to insure that these books would be translated into Latin for the public benefit of our faith and at the time of his death, three of them had already appeared. The Hebrews hold these same books in such reverence that no one under forty years of age is permitted even to touch them. I acquired these books at considerable expense and, reading them from beginning to end with the greatest attention and with unrelenting toil, I discovered in them (as God is my witness) not so much the Mosaic as the Christian religion. There was to be found the mystery of the Trinity, the Incarnation of the

Word, the divinity of the Messiah; there one might also read of original sin, of its expiation by Christ, of the heavenly Jerusalem, of the fall of the demons, of the orders of the angels, of the pains of purgatory and of hell. There I read the same things which we read every day in the pages of Paul and of Dionysius, Jerome and Augustine. In philosophical matters, it were as though one were listening to Pythagoras and Plato, whose doctrines bear so close an affinity to the Christian faith that our Augustine offered endless thanks to God that the books of the Platonists had fallen into his hands.[46] In a word, there is no point of controversy between the Hebrews and ourselves on which the Hebrews cannot be confuted and convinced out of the cabalistic writings, so that no corner is left for them to hide in. On this point I can cite a witness of the very greatest authority, the most learned Antonius Chronicus; on the occasion of a banquet in his house, at which I was also present, with his own ears he heard the Hebrew, Dactylus, a profound scholar of this lore, come round completely to the Christian doctrine of the Trinity.

To return, however, to our review of the chief points of my disputation: I have also adduced my conception of the manner in which the poems of Orpheus and Zoroaster ought to be interpreted. Orpheus is read by the Greeks in a text which is practically complete; Zoroaster is known to them in a corrupt text, while in Chaldea he is read in a form more nearly complete. Both are considered as the authors and fathers of ancient wisdom. I shall say nothing about Zoroaster who is mentioned frequently by the Platonists and always with the greatest respect. Of Pythagoras, however, Iamblicus the Chaldean writes that he took the Orphic theology as the model on which he shaped and formed his own philosophy. For this precise reason the sayings of Pythagoras are called sacred, because, and to the degree that, they derive from the Orphic teachings. For from this source that occult doctrine of numbers and everything

66

else that was great and sublime in Greek
philosophy flowed as from its primitive
source. Orpheus, however, (and this was
the case with all the ancient theologians)
so wove the mysteries of his doctrines into
the fabric of myths and so wrapped them
about in veils of poetry, that one reading
his hymns might well believe that there
was nothing in them but fables and the
veriest commonplaces. I have said this so
that it might be known what labor was
mine, what difficulty was involved, in
drawing out the secret meanings of the
occult philosophy from the deliberate tan-
gles of riddles and the recesses of fable in
which they were hidden; difficulty made
all the greater by the fact that in a matter
so weighty, abstruse and unexplored, I
could count on no help from the work and
efforts of other interpreters. And still like
dogs they have come barking after me,
saying that I have brought together an ac-
cumulation of trifles in order to make a
great display by their sheer number. As
though all did not concern ambiguous

questions, subjects of sharpest controversy, over which the most important schools confront each other like gladiators. As though I had not brought to light many things quite unknown and unsuspected by these very men who now carp at me while styling themselves the leaders of philosophy. As a matter of fact, I am so completely free of the fault they attribute to me that I have tried to confine the discussion to fewer points than I might have raised. Had I wished, (as others are wont) to divide these questions into their constituent parts, and to dismember them, their number might well have increased to a point past counting. To say nothing of other matters, who is unaware that one of these nine hundred theses, that, namely, concerning the reconciliation of the philosophies of Plato and Aristotle might have been developed, without arousing any suspicion that I was affecting mere number, into six hundred or more by enumerating in due order those points on which others think that these philosophies differ and I, that they agree? For a certainty I shall speak out (though in a manner which is neither modest in itself nor conformable to my character), I shall speak out because those who envy me and detract me, force me to speak out. I have wanted to make clear in this disputation, not only that I know a great many things, but also that I know a great many things which others do not know.

And now, reverend Fathers, in order that this claim may be vindicated by the fact, and in order that my address may no longer delay the satisfaction of your desire —for I see, reverend doctors, with the greatest pleasure that you are girded and ready for the contest—let us now, with the prayer that the outcome may be fortunate and favorable, as to the sound of war-trumpets, join battle.

NOTES

1. Probably 'Abd-Allah Ibn al Muqaffa (718-775 A.D.), noted for his translations of Medo-Persian writings into Arabic.
2. Asclepius I, 6a (*Hermetica,* ed. Scott, I, 294)
3. Psalms VIII, 6
4. Genesis II, 1; Plato *Timaeus* 41b
5. Lucilius, Frag. 623 (ed. Marx, Leipzig, 1904)
6. For justification of transliteration cf. Cicognani, *op. cit.,* pp. 97-98.
7. Enoch 40:8
8. As with many proper names in Pico, scholars have not been able to identify this Euanthes (Evanthes) with certainty.
9. Cf. note 6 above and Cicognani *op. cit.,* pp. 12-13.
10. Psalms LXXXII, 6
11. Cf. Dionysius *On the Celestial Hierarchy* VII.
12. Job 38:7
13. Genesis 28:12
14. Job 25:2
15. Frag. 115, 13-14 (ed. Diels)
16. Paraphrased from Matthew 11:28 or John 14:27
17. Plato *Phaedo* 81a
18. Cf. Exodus 26:14; 36:19; 39:33 and Cicognani, pp. 105-106.

19. Plato *Phaedrus* 245b
20. Recalls Rom. 1:20
21. Reminiscent of John 1:9
22. Plato *Alcibiades* 133c
23. Plato *Phaedo* 118a
24. Psalms LV, 18; St. Augustine *De Genesi ad litteram* IV, 47
25. Jeremiah 9:21
26. Cf. Cicognani, *op. cit.*, pp. 112-113.
27. Job 32:8
28. 1 Tim. 4:12
29. *De Finibus* I, 1
30. Propertius II, 10, 5-6
31. Horace *Epistles* I, 1, 14
32. The philosophers referred to are: Duns Scotus (d. 1308); St. Thomas Aquinas (1224-1274); Giles of Rome (1246?-1316); Franciscus of Mayronis (?-1327); St. Albert the Great (1193-1280); Henry of Ghent (d. 1293); Averroës (d. 1198); Avempace (1138); Alfarabi (d. 950); Simplicius (fl. circa 530); Themistius (fl. circa 350); Alexander of Aphrodisias (fl. circa 200); the others are for the most part neo-platonists. The list constitutes a selection from those mentioned in Pico's nine-hundred propositions. Cf. further Runes, *Dictionary of Philosophy* (New York, 1944) *passim*.
33. Plato *Epistles* VII, 341c-d

34. "Asymboli": those who contributed nothing to the cost of a banquet at which they partook.
35. Seneca *Epistles* XXXIII, 7
36. St. Augustine, *Contra Academicos* III, 42
37. Plato *Epinomis* 976c
38. Aristotle *Problems* CCCI, 6, 956a
39. Plato *Republic* 525b
40. Plato *Alcibiades* 122a
41. Plato *Charmides* 1562, 157a
42. Al-Kindi (d. circa 870); Roger Bacon (d. 1294); William of Paris, known better as William of Auvergne (d. 1249)
43. Hilary of Poitiers "The Athanasius of the West" (d. 306); Origen (185-254)
44. *Ecclus.* 46:1
45. *Esdras* II, 14:5-6
46. e.g. *Confessions* VII, 2

Gateway Editions

ANSKY, S., *The Dybbuk*
AQUINAS, ST. THOMAS, *An Introduction to Metaphysics*
AQUINAS, ST. THOMAS, *Treatise on Law*
AUGUSTINE, ST., *Enchiridion on Faith, Hope and Love*
AUGUSTINE, ST., *The Political Writings*
BIERCE, AMBROSE, *Ambrose Bierce's Civil War*
BOETHIUS, *The Consolation of Philosophy*
BUCKLEY, WILLIAM F., JR., *God and Man at Yale*
BURKE, EDMUND, *Selected Writings*
BURNHAM, JAMES, *The Machiavellians*
BURNHAM, JAMES, *Suicide of the West*
CHAMBERS, WHITTAKER, *Odyssesy of a Friend*
CHAMBERS, WHITTAKER, *Witness*
CLAUSEWITZ, KARL von, *War, Politics, and Power*
CROSSMAN, RICHARD H., *The God That Failed*
CUSTINE, MARQUIS de, *A Journey for Our Time*
FREUD, SIGMUND, *The Origin and Development of Psychoanalysis*
GUARDINI, ROMANO, *The Lord*
HEIDEGGER, MARTIN, *Existence and Being*
HITTI, PHILIP K., *The Arabs: A Short History*
KIRK, RUSSELL, *The Conservative Mind*
LOCKE, JOHN, *The Reasonableness of Christianity*
MARX, KARL, *The Communist Manifesto*
MARX, KARL, *Das Kapital*
MASTROBUONO, ANTONIO C., *Dante's Journey of Sanctification*
MENCKEN, H.L., *H.L. Mencken's Smart Set Criticism*
NIETZSCHE, FRIEDRICH, *Philosophy in the Tragic Age of the Greeks*
PICARD, MAX, *The Flight from God*
PICO della MIRANDOLA, GIOVANNI, *Oration on the Dignity of Man*
PLATO, *Euthyphro, Crito, Apology, and Symposium*
RYN, CLAES, *Will, Imagination and Reason*
SARTRE, JEAN-PAUL, *Existential Psychoanalysis*
SOSEKI, NATSUME, *Kokoro*
SOSEKI, NATSUME, *Three Cornered World*
STEVENSON, ROBERT LOUIS, *Selected Essays*
UNAMUNO, MIGUEL de, *Abel Sanchez*
VOEGELIN, ERIC, *Science, Politics, and Gnosticism*
MISES, LUDWIG von, *Economic Policy*